The Mentoring Manual

What I've Learned over 50 years of Mentoring

Todd Dorsey

THE MENTORING MANUAL

Please direct all copyright inquiries to:
B.O.Y. Enterprises, Inc
P.O. Box 262
Lowell, NC 28098

Paperback ISBN: 978-1-955605-50-2

Interior Design: B.O.Y. Enterprises, Inc.

Printed in the United States.

Dedication

This book is dedicated to all the men and women who sacrifice their time and ambitions to reach back to bring others up with them.

"Things that have been confirmed by reliable witnesses. Now teach these truths to other trustworthy people who will be able to pass them on to others." **-II Timothy 2:2 (NLT)**

Acknowledgements

I would like to thank God for giving me the strength to be a model, the courage to stand out, and the inspiration to motivate young people. I thank my wife Myra for the love, sacrifice, and understanding of allowing me to have an impact.

Thank you to my children Myranda, Ashley, and Deidre for unwavering commitments to pursue their purpose, and allowing me to share my time.

I thank my mother, Annie Dorsey, for letting me go and trusting me to make good decisions, and surrounding me with Mentors and positive socializations.

Thanks go to Otescia Johnson, Author, for coaching me and guiding my journey on this project.

Thank you Deidre Dorsey for cover design and graphics, Ann Pierce for typing, and J. Snapp photography for author pictures.

Special thanks and dedications go to:

Rev. James Smith, Mr. Haywood Homesley, Rev. Frankie Smith of Shelby , NC.

The families of the late Dr. Don C. Locke, and Dr. Thomas H. Conway of NSCU, and Mr. Herbert Sneed.

Table of Contents

TEENAGERS AND BEHAVIOR 6

MENTORS 8

TIME 10

SEVEN HABITS 12

CONSISTENCY 14

BE FLEXIBLE 16

AVAILABILITY 21

BE A MODEL 25

BE AN EXTENSION OF THE PARENT 28

MULTI-CULTURAL MENTORING 31

About the Author 35

TEENAGERS AND BEHAVIOR

"A hundred years from now… It will not matter what kind of car I drove, what kind of house I lived in, or how much money I had in my bank account, but the world may be better because I was important in the life of a child." -**Forest Witcraft**

The one constant thing I have shown in working with teenagers is that they will display new behaviors and discontinue other pre-teen behaviors, based on the attention given to them. If the behavior is rewarded in his or her environment peer groups such as a teenager interested in devoting his/her time to athletics, may decide to stop any substance or tobacco use. At the same time, another youth may begin the same substance use or smoking behaviors, just to fit in with a specific peer group. The behavior may be low because he/she had not had previous peer interactions that accepted or awarded those actions.

Generally, teens are copycats. They will experiment and value actions based on the peer group he/she seeks to become involved with. A child may have been quiet and introverted as a pre-teen but in high school they decided to change peer groups, due to geographics, a family move, other friend's moves or simply changes in his/her personality or physical growth.

In my observation, it is rare for an extraverted child to become more introverted as a teenager/ adolescent. It is more likely for an introverted or quiet child to increase social/peer interactions as a teen, thus, becoming more extroverted as an adolescent. It is also rare for an adolescent to behave differently than his/her peer group. If the peer group values good grades, he or she will value making good grades. The opposite is also true. At some stage in the development, an adolescent will make good grades or even see their academics decrease based on peer interactions.

If an adolescent hang around peers who makes good grades in school, he/she may not have the same associations in the community. Likewise, peers in the community may not be the peer group he/she decides to associate within the school environment. In no way do adolescents want to be an outsider while on a high school campus. By and large, athletes associate with athletes, computer geeks with computer geeks, preppies with preppies, pot head smokers with smokers and the list goes on.

The school day is too long and you are much too _____ to not feel comfortable with a peer group. One may ask "*what about the child who is a loner?*" My response would be that the loner will interact or gravitate to other students who are considered loners.

Show me your peers and you'll show me your future.

MENTORS

Mentors are individuals who are active in our lives for a specific purpose and during a specific period of time.

Mentors are not designed to appoint nor to "*not*" appoint, to take the place of parents. They are to aid and reinforce parenting. They also may be asked to fill a void in a specific area of development, where a parent may be less knowledgeable. This is especially apparent, when there is a child from a single-parent household. A mentor is asked to fill a void, model and teach manhood.

Mentors should not be viewed as a "Be all or End all". In other words, mentors have limited skills and knowledge as well. For example, an athletic coach may not necessarily be the right fit for mentoring on relationships, finances, auto mechanic, or spiritual matters. However, a spiritual leader may be a great mentor in church, (spiritually and with relationships), but not necessarily effective in physical or health- related development.

Mentors should not feel as though they should be an expert on all matters. "Stay in your lane!". If you don't have the expertise in a particular area, seek other adults or resources to provide that knowledge. If a child has an interest in medicine or healthcare, (unless you're a medical professional), it would be recommended for you to seek and introduce that child to a medical professional. Likewise, if a child is experiencing educational problems, unless you're academically inclined, you may not be the best match for the child.

It is important for an adult mentor to not only know his or her strengths but to also understand their limitations. Mentors are due more psychological changes, by attempting to portray an image they are not.

"Life is about making an impact; not making an income"

Kevin Kruse

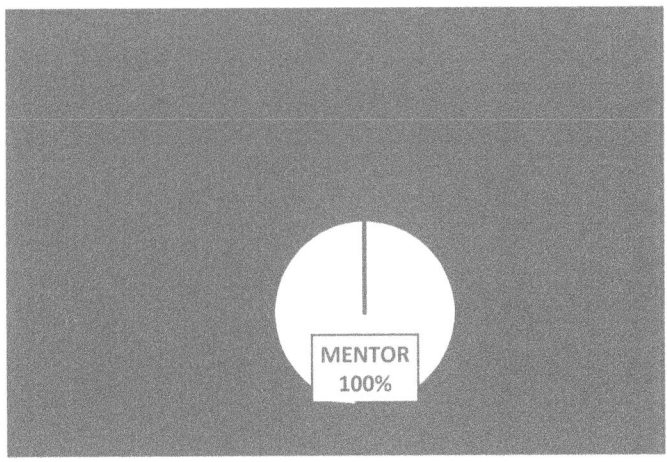

TIME

It takes time to model and mentor. I have witnessed many individuals seeking to become mentors because they were excited in a moment and really sought to give back to the community by helping a child. They later found out that the time needed to make an impact is much more than they can give.

Let's say you agreed to give 2 hours per week and early on, there were no issues or conflicts. But as the relationship progressed, the child discloses more about the difficulties or challenges he or she is experiencing. The adult mentor then begins to think the situation requires more time than he or she can give. They decide to back off a bit. The child then becomes frustrated and no longer wants the relationship to continue because of the adult's inconsistency.

I suggest you commit to the minimum amount of time. Youths have too many other hobbies and activities to become enjoyed in. If your activities are not as compelling as their normal activities, this then results in just another failed relationship and will be less likely to be effective to any other mentor type activity.

Shock and disappointment are real emotional responses during an unemployment incident. Especially when you didn't see it coming. You just literally stand still as though someone had died. Well, someone has died; that person was you. Though you're still alive, a part of you dies. Your character has been assassinated, your hopes have been delayed, your dreams cut short, and motivation halted.

"Strive not to be a success, but rather to be of value."

Albert Einstein

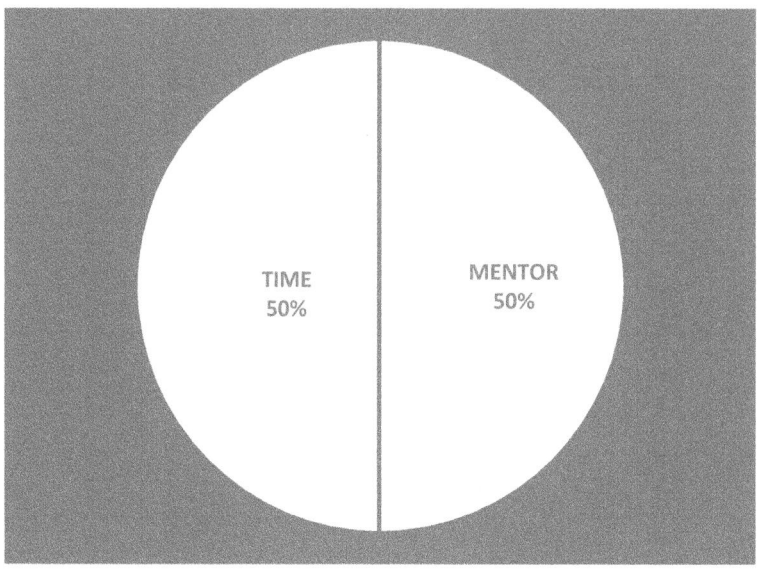

SEVEN HABITS

The discipline of mentoring has become a big word and took over the past 20 years than it even has. The word has been around forever but now it's a priority. Some view mentoring as a temporary task while others view it as a lifelong relationship.

My purpose is to point out several characteristics I think are the most important. These are, by no means, an exhaustive list. My list is based on more than 40 years of youthwork. My hope is that you will find where you fit in, take these traits and apply them to your relationships and become a more effective leader and teacher. After all, that's what a mentor is… A teacher, not in an academic book sense, but a teacher in life. To help someone think of other approaches to life, they would not have considered before. A mentor is not a "do as I say" but a "do as I do" kind of teacher. I will talk more about this later.

"The best time to plant a tree was 20 years ago. The second-best time is now"

Chinese Proverb

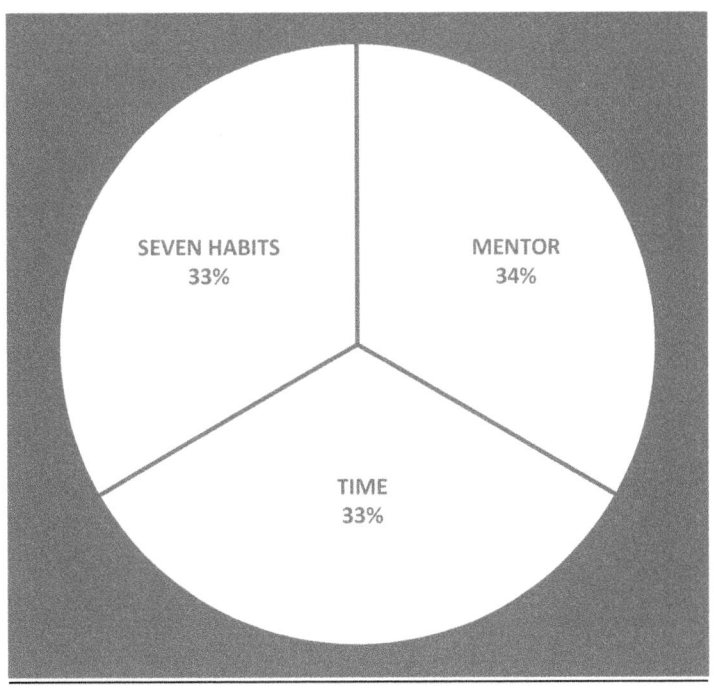

CONSISTENCY

Being consistent is primary. A lot of people start out being excited about mentoring. It's a priority but something happens to cause the adult to pull from the commitment. Being a mentor IS a commitment.

I have known and seen adults who start out with lots of excitement and dedication. But the relationship becomes more demanding based on a child's behavior and life demands. If you commit to 2 times per week, be consistent with these 2 sessions. A child and the parent know it takes at least twice a week; you will be there.

"Every child is an artist. The problem is how to remain an artist once he grows up."

Pablo Picasso

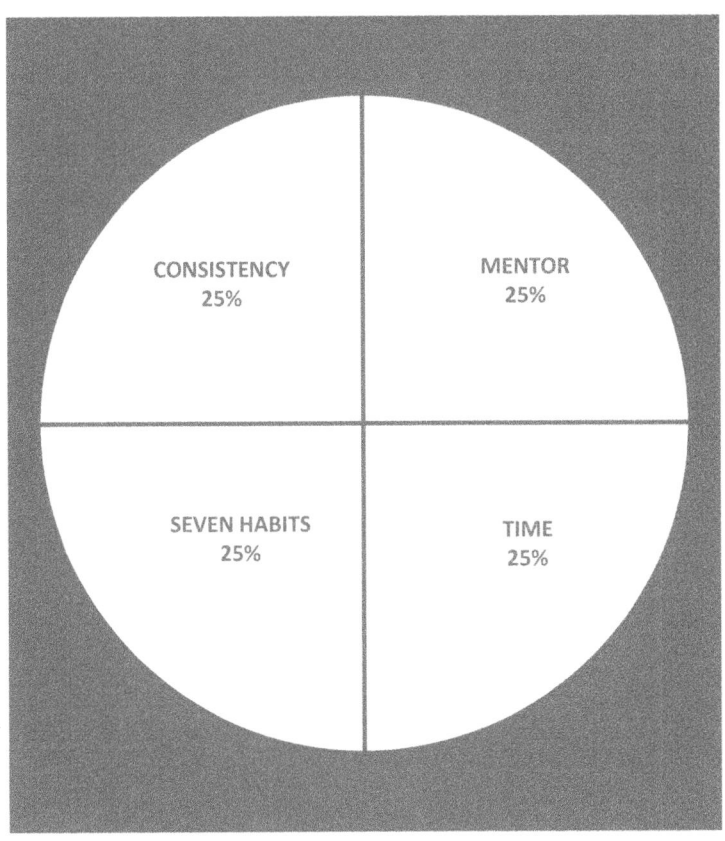

BE FLEXIBLE

The mentor will learn just as much from being in the child's environment as the child learns from observing you. Let's say you begin the interaction by taking the child to the mall. After several visits, the child is not as excited as before. In conversation, you learn that he or she enjoys going to the park or just being outdoors. You discover the child likes being around water or likes fishing. You on the other hand, have no interest in fishing as an activity. This is where the child becomes the teacher. He can expose you to a life you are not familiar with. Or let's say you take the child to go play basketball. You love basketball. It is a popular sport and is always a conversation topic in any social environment. However, over a period of time, you discover the child would rather play soccer. You are still the teacher and mentor because you still model learning, self-control and effort.

The beauty of being a mentor role model is to expose the child to environments that he or she would not normally have access to. Of course, you begin the relationship with making the child comfortable with you in his or her own environment. Never have the child think his or her environment is not as valuable and resourceful as other environments. Don't get into the habit of taking the child out of their comfort zone. If you choose to play basketball, begin with going to a gymnasium or park in close proximity to the child's home or school. One of the goals of being a mentor is to expose the child to many positive environments as possible. But if that environment is not accessible anytime you are not present, there could be a problem. The mentor creates a positive within the child's immediate environment, then branch out into other environments.

You may place a high value on the location and the child will eventually do the same. But he or she may not be as excited early on. When you're around, the child feels safe, excited and empowered. But when you are not available, or the child does not have access to those gyms, parks or malls; how does the child capture that same feeling of excitement or positive like? That's why you should always first begin to empower youths in their immediate environment. So, when you are not around, they can still experience a level of accomplishment on their own. The sense of purpose is the direct result of the established relationship, not the place. The approach should be to make the child comfortable in the interaction, then branch out to new environments. I suggest you build up to the grand and new experiences.

Let me give another example: Let's say you decide to take the child out to eat. You are thinking "what a great experience it would be to go to Ruth Chris Steakhouse, Cheesecake Factory or Outback Steakhouse". Granted, these are fabulous eating restaurants and as exciting as it would be, the child may feel totally lost in such environments. It may be more meaningful to start with going to McDonald's or Burger King. This is what a child may be most familiar with and comfortable in. He or she will talk more and likely self-discipline as opposed to larger, grand restaurants. I guarantee, you will get more conversation from a child at a school cafeteria or McDonald's, than a larger, high dollar establishment.

Again, the goal is to begin with the small and the familiar. Then branch out to the new and unfamiliar. It's better to begin small and grow large, rather than begin large and drop down. Always think about ways to create the feeling of anticipation. The new and the next are the sea salt of relationship growth. The time with you is much more valuable than the place or environment.

The new experiences should be earned based on how well the child behaves in the smaller, familiar environments. Don't bite off more than you can chew. Begin with what's realistic and familiar.

You as a mentor will learn more about the child and their experiences by engaging with them in "their" world. Be wary of thinking, you are a hero who is just there to "save the child." You are simply there to teach, model, and enrich.

As I mentioned before, the child is also the teacher; you can learn just as much from being exposed to their world. For example, years ago I was mentoring an 11-year-old youngster. At the end of our time, I would drop him off at his mother's job. Her job was in a high traffic area of the city. I'm sure my frustrations began to show every time I dropped him off. I regularly complained about sitting in traffic to and from the location.

On this particular day, the youngster asked "Mr. Todd, have you ever thought about riding the light rail?" Well, I had not thought about that; after all, why would I? I had my own vehicle and didn't need to use the light rail. So, anyway, we began to ride the light rail from downtown Charlotte to his mother's job, 8 miles away. Wow, what a great idea! What a great learning experience. This changed our whole interaction and dialogue. He was much more excited about riding the light rail, than he was with riding in my vehicle. It saved time and gasoline. It eliminated the traffic stress and we got to talk more.

I learned more about him and I'm sure he learned more about me. In fact, I learned more from him in this experience. He became the teacher, the mentor and the guide. I'm sure he felt empowered by exposing me to the public transportation. Needless to say, I began to ride the light rail many more times after that and even introduced it to *my* adult peers. As a mentor, he was ready and opened to learn. Not only will the youth be introduced to *your* world, you will be introduced to theirs as well.

"I've learned that people will forget what you said, people will forget what you did, but people will never forget how you made them feel"

Maya Angelou

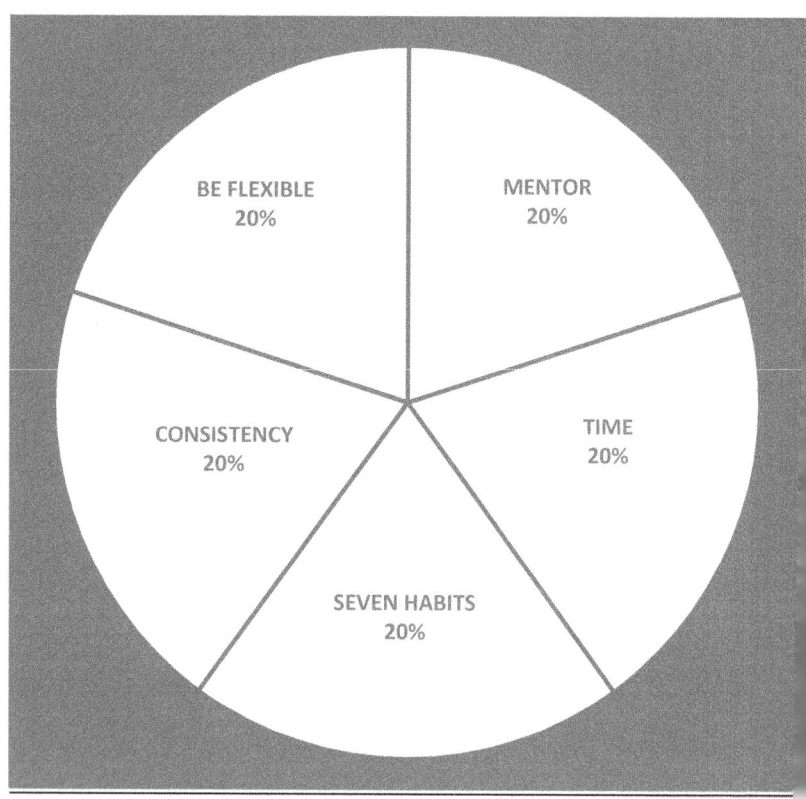

AVAILABILITY

It will be up to you to determine how available and accessible you will be. You have established an honest and trustworthy relationship. You are now a part of their support system. Expect phone calls from time to time. The child or family will call you to seek advice to inform you of an accomplished task, to check on you and "yes", when a problem arises. Every interaction will not require you to leave your area but will require verbal interaction.

You are a new fresh and knowledgeable resource that the family may have never had. I've known mentors who limit the interaction to an assigned time. If you don't want to be interrupted during certain times such as, lunch, after-school programs or a weekend, let that be established early on. Your feedback and opinions are important to the child you are mentoring.

Let's say you are assisting with schoolwork and assignments and the child may let you know of a test, exam or research paper project that is due. Or, if the child is involved in an extra-curricular activity like sports, band, clubs or a church youth group, he or she will inform you of a game, trip or activity. That is their way of saying "I would like for you to be there."

Some youths may come from a family where the parent cannot or does not have time to give attention outside of the home. This is where you step in as a "pseudo" parent or a parent substitute. You are not a parent replacement; you are simply a substitute. But, to have you present will be life changing and very meaningful to the child. You now have been exposed to "their" world. You also now have another frame of reference to refer to, during your conversation with the child of the family. You can help guide the child further in their extracurricular interests. This allows you to open the child up to a whole new world of opportunities.

You have permission to introduce the child/family to other resources or activities that they have not had access to. You now can encourage the child to excel in the extracurricular interest. This could be the past time activity that keeps them active, out of trouble and a reason to hope and dream. The activity is their way out of negative peer or community behaviors. If the child plays a sport, you can introduce them to a similar sports/athletic program after the school season ends. There may be a church league or athletic association to participate in. However, if you introduce them to the extended activity, you have obligated yourself as their means of transportation.

So again, you must determine your level of involvement and how available you wish to be. It's possible that the parent may choose to take over and assist you in the new role. Even if they don't, you are obligated to inform them of all activities you are getting the child involved in.

Let's say the child plays an instrument, you can now introduce him or her to other community arts activities. Hopefully you have arranged activity to where there is no cost for the parent. If there is a cost and you choose to pay it, you have now opened yourself up to another level of expectations.

You have knowledge of a dynamic youth group for the child. You choose to involve the child in this group. Again, you have obligated yourself to be responsible for transportation. I don't see any parent objecting to increased interactions. However, whatever you start, you are committed to finish.

"What do you do if a child needs an outlet but does not know what they are interested in?"

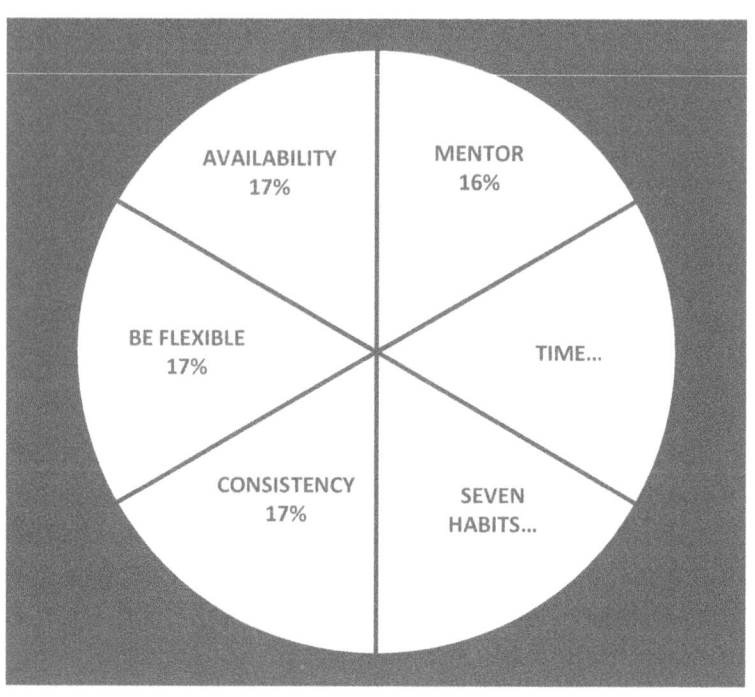

BE A MODEL

The sole purpose of you being a mentor is for you to model the behaviors, activities and interactions you are attempting to portray to the child. It is my hope and belief that you have enough life experiences or resources, which have equipped you with skills and coping mechanism that prepared you for a successful adulthood.

The child has been identified as needing a mentor, coach role model, based on professional opinion of the parent, educator, courts or community leader. They have observed a behavioral pattern that says he or she needs additional guidance in a particular area. Your primary task is to model the behavior.

Being a successful mentor does not require perfection, but it does require professionalism. Professionalism means you conduct your behavior in such a way as to say *"watch what I do more than what I say."* If a child has an issue with anger management, he or she should not observe inappropriate anger outbursts from a mentor. To observe negative responses from a mentor will only validate the child's negative behavior.

A mentor will be able to observe a child's reactions and behaviors in many areas. You are able to communicate in ways other adults in his or her life cannot, because you have direct access to his or her thoughts and behavior. The mentor role is less restricted and fewer boundaries.

The child observes how you interact with the world. He will model that behavior the next time he or she is in a similar situation. Your behavior validates their behavior. You are now the filler and measuring stick for their information. As I said before, as a mentor, you have to count the cost and decide how much time and emotion you want to invest in the relationship. You could just be in the child's life for an appointed time. After that time has expired, your assignment has been completed. On the other hand, you may decide to maintain the relationship for a longer period of time. Even after the assignment has expired, the lessons and skills learned, will last the child's lifetime. You just have to decide how much you want to disclose of yourself.

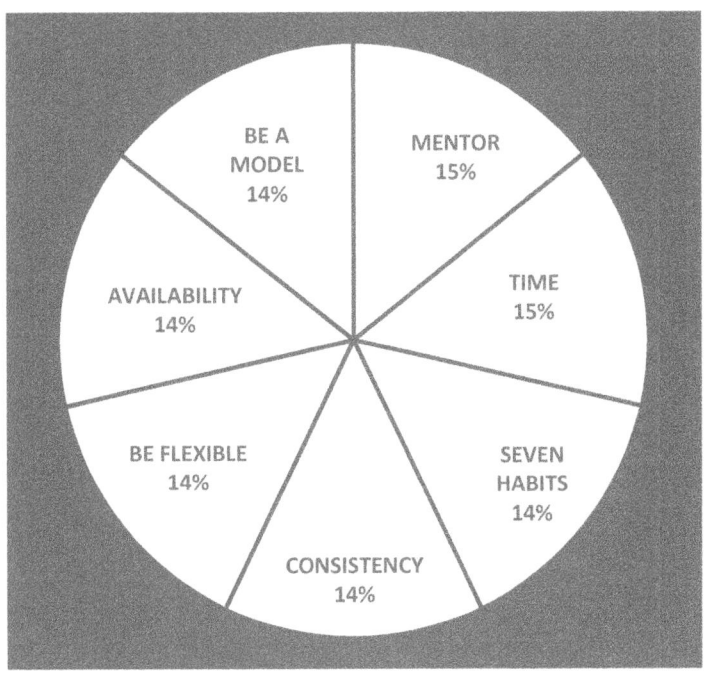

BE AN EXTENSION OF THE PARENT

Effective mentors understand they are not the parent and do not take place of the parent. Effective mentors understand they are simply an extension of the parent. You are to reinforce the decisions and parenting rules already set in place. This is why it is so important to establish and maintain open communication with the parent. You are a temporary assignment. Parenting is more effective mentors needed to understand they are there to fill a void and to provide guidance the child may be lacking in a particular area.

Even when relating to school or community personnel, let it be known that you will communicate all information to the child's parent. Your assignment is not to become the person the child turns to, as an escape from reality.

For example, let's say the child has broken a rule at home, school or in the community. If the parent decides to issue a consequence for the behavior, you as a mentor should support the parent's decision. A mentor is not to make life easier for the child. If the child views you as "everything that's good" and sees they can bypass their parents, the child will do just that.

Children are children for a reason. Children do best what children do most and that is, how can I change or manipulate these adults. Even though you are spending your precious time, talent and resources with this child, you are not exempt from their "game playing". Children play games. Children are good at playing games. Adolescents are masters at this game. This is why it is very important for you as a mentor to communicate with other adults in the child's life.

Most children don't like structure and rules. But children should have structure and rules. Nothing influences behavior like structures and rules do. However, one thing we know about youths is they don't want rules or structure.

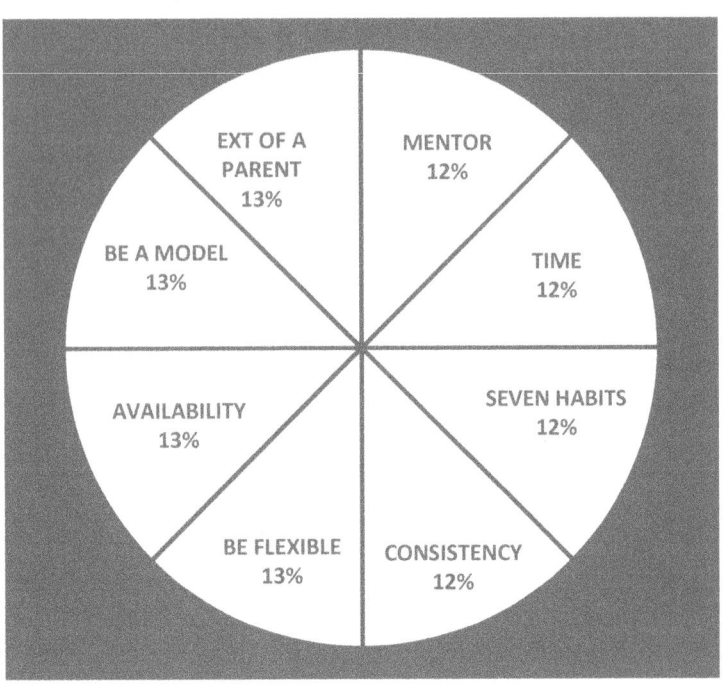

MULTI-CULTURAL MENTORING

This section deserves its own book. There is not enough time or space to address the importance and significance of the multi-cultural mentoring relationships. However, I will attempt to address the matter to provide a springboard for discussion and for the reader/mentor to always be aware of culture.

I am not aware of any research that supports likeness in culture, as a guarantee for success in a mentoring relationship. While it may be ideal for the mentor/mentee relationship be of the same culture, it may *not* be realistic or advantageous. Being of the same culture does have positives and can eliminate barriers in the relationship. The mentor/child (mentee) relationship can indeed be of the same culture and still be problematic, because there are many layers of culture within the culture. For example, let's say the child is African American and the mentor is African American as well. On the surface, this appears to be an ideal match. However, there are other cultural differences within the African American community.

The same can be said of the Caucasian, Asian, Hispanic and Latin communities, as well as other multi-racial communities. You as a mentor must be comfortable and competent of your own culture first. Then and only then, will you be able to be comfortable in a multi-cultural dialogue.

Differences in culture does create a great opportunity for learning and increased dialogue. As I stated earlier, the mentor must be willing to learn. Culture changes and sub-groups change within their cultures. The values, communication and lifestyles of all cultures have changed over the years and are continually evolving each day. The plight of today's adolescent or young adults is totally different from the lifestyle of when we were at that age. Communication, multi-media and transportation has changed, where there are (as an example), many more adolescents owning their own vehicles these days. Entertainment and our concept of play and pastime activities are different, including the communities that we live in. My point is just because you are from the same cultural or racial group, does not mean you had the same life experiences.

I was at one of our local malls this past week and walked pass an African American owned barbershop. I observed that all of the barbers there were African-American. However, I noticed the ones waiting in line were 5 to 6 White and Hispanic families (youths). So, what do we know about the African-American barbershop? It is one of the most interactive environments in the African-American community. This is where we get updated information on the latest fashion, music trends, sporting events and political insight. The latest gossip is affirmed or refuted in African-American barbershops of which some of my best arguments have either won or lost in a conversation. In fact, if you can withstand opposing opinions in the barbershop, your views are officially validated.

Here are these Caucasian and Hispanic families in this African American barbershop, not only will they receive a "fresh cut", but they will also receive valuable advice from conversations on school, sports, music and life skills. That environment has built-in mentorship. Think about your barbershop or hair stylist experiences and the feelings, emotions and communication patterns which took place. This environment has been known as a "note of passage" in the African-American male development.

Now families from other cultures are taking advantage of that experience. We are much more multi-cultural today than we ever have been, as a society. We are more alike than different and are more willing to learn and be exposed to other cultures. The more comfortable you are with your own and other cultures, will dictate how effective you can be in a multi-cultural mentoring relationship.

As a mentor, I encourage you to seek out and pursue opportunities to expose youths and young adults to other cultures. Many of them know very little of other cultural environments, outside of the school settings. Highly effective mentors are multi-culturally minded.

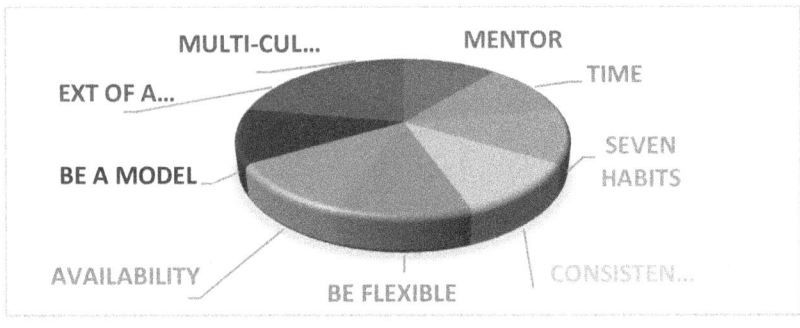

About the Author

Todd Dorsey is a native of Shelby, North Carolina. He was reared in a single parent household with 4 sisters and brothers. His young life was filled with a love and passion for athletics. He went on to letter in 3 sports in High School, where he was on 3 state championship teams, and president of his senior class. Todd went on to earn undergraduate and graduate degrees from North Carolina Stated University in Raleigh, NC. He has over 30 years in the Social Work and Mental Health Profession. Todd has developed, coordinated, and participated in numerous programs designed to reach and complete the at risk and inner-city youth. He credits athletics for keeping him focused and directing him to higher aspirations. He credits his mother and his many coaches and mentors for helping develop his accomplishments. He and wife, Myra, now reside in Charlotte, NC, and have 3 adult children.